Let's Investigate with Nate

Dinosaurs

Written by **Nate Ball** • Illustrated by **Wes Hargis**

HARPER
An Imprint of HarperCollinsPublishers

For Cat, who makes the impossible possible

Dear Reader,

Dinosaurs!

I've found dinosaurs fascinating since I was little and loved imagining meeting one in real life. Imagine looking up, suddenly seeing the head of a sauropod rising over you! The ground shakes as it takes a step, its body almost as big as a city bus balanced ten feet overhead on legs the size of tree trunks.

As amazing as dinosaurs themselves is that we know so much about them. Unlike other sciences where you can directly observe what you're studying, we learn about dinosaurs by the clues they left behind. This is the scientific field of **paleontology.**

Paleontology is powerful because it lets us learn so much from so little. It helps us understand what the world was like when dinosaurs lived—and it helps us understand what our world might be like in the future.

In this book, I imagined what it would be like to learn about dinosaurs and their habitats by directly observing them. If you went along with the investigators on this adventure, what might you observe? And how does that change what you observe in the world around you now? I hope you enjoy the challenge!

Your friend,

Nate

Let's Investigate with Nate: Dinosaurs
Text copyright © 2018 by Nate Ball
Illustrations copyright © 2018 by Wes Hargis
All rights reserved. Manufactured in China.
No part of this book may be used or reproduced in any manner whatsoever without written permission except in the case of brief quotations embodied in critical articles and reviews. For information address HarperCollins Children's Books, a division of HarperCollins Publishers, 195 Broadway, New York, NY 10007.
www.harpercollinschildrens.com
Library of Congress Control Number: 2017949548
ISBN 978-0-06-235746-5 (trade bdg.)—ISBN 978-0-06-235745-8 (pbk.)

The artist used pencils and digital paint to create the illustrations for this book.
Typography by Erica De Chavez
18 19 20 21 22 SCP 10 9 8 7 6 5 4 3 2 1
❖
First Edition

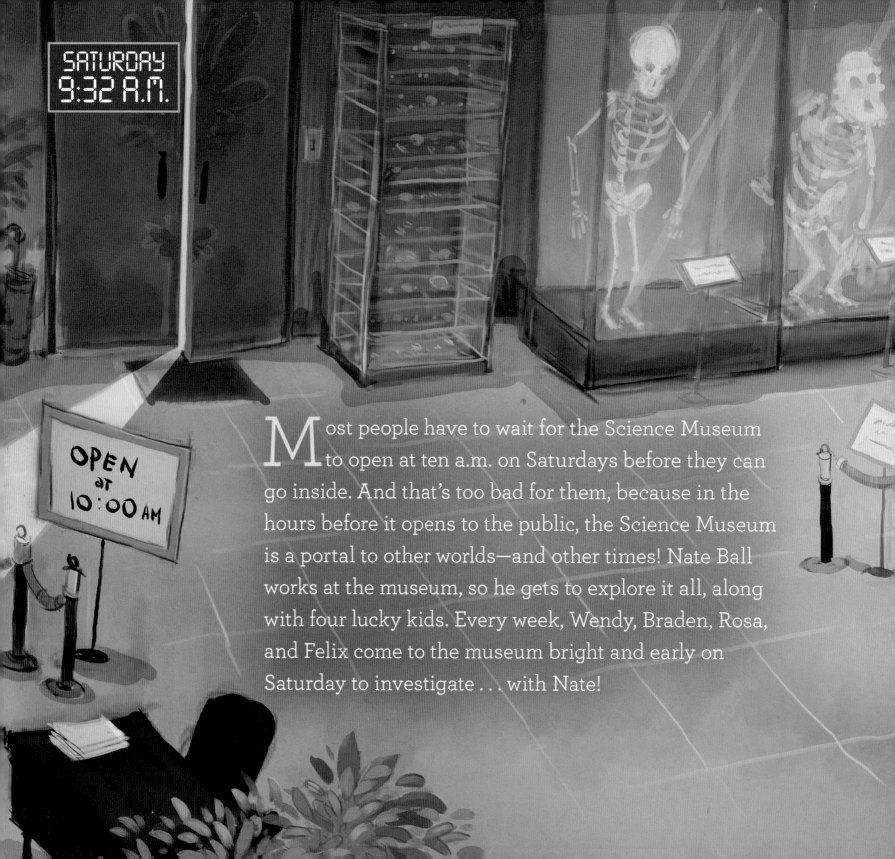

SATURDAY 9:32 A.M.

OPEN at 10:00 AM

Most people have to wait for the Science Museum to open at ten a.m. on Saturdays before they can go inside. And that's too bad for them, because in the hours before it opens to the public, the Science Museum is a portal to other worlds—and other times! Nate Ball works at the museum, so he gets to explore it all, along with four lucky kids. Every week, Wendy, Braden, Rosa, and Felix come to the museum bright and early on Saturday to investigate . . . with Nate!

It can be hard to wrap your head around the history of Earth. We know it's 4.5 billion years old, but what does that mean? And how can we know what Earth was like 4.5 billion years ago? Anything that was around that long ago *died* long ago.

So how do we learn about Earth's history?

Fossils.

Fossils are the preserved remains of long-dead creatures. When these creatures' remains become fossilized, they become as hard as rock. This is why fossils last so long. People have found fossils of tiny bacteria that are almost as old as the earth itself.

BRADEN'S JOURNAL
Compared to the lifetime of our planet, humans haven't been around that long—just 200,000 years. If you think of Earth's whole life as one day, humans have only been around for the last minute!

Dinosaur fossils are some of the most famous fossils around. Much of what we know about dinosaurs we've learned from studying their fossils. **Paleontologists** can tell a lot about dinosaurs from just a few bits of preserved bone. A paleontologist might look at bite marks in the bones of one dinosaur to see what kind of meat-eating dinosaur killed it. Or she might check out the fossils in other rocks near dinosaur fossils to see what kind of plants the dinosaurs lived around. You'd be amazed at how much we can learn just from fossils!

Dinosaurs are ancient animals who lived on Earth for hundreds of millions of years. The last **non-avian** dinosaurs went extinct around sixty-six million years ago, but nobody's exactly sure why they all died. Many scientists think it happened after a giant asteroid hit Earth.

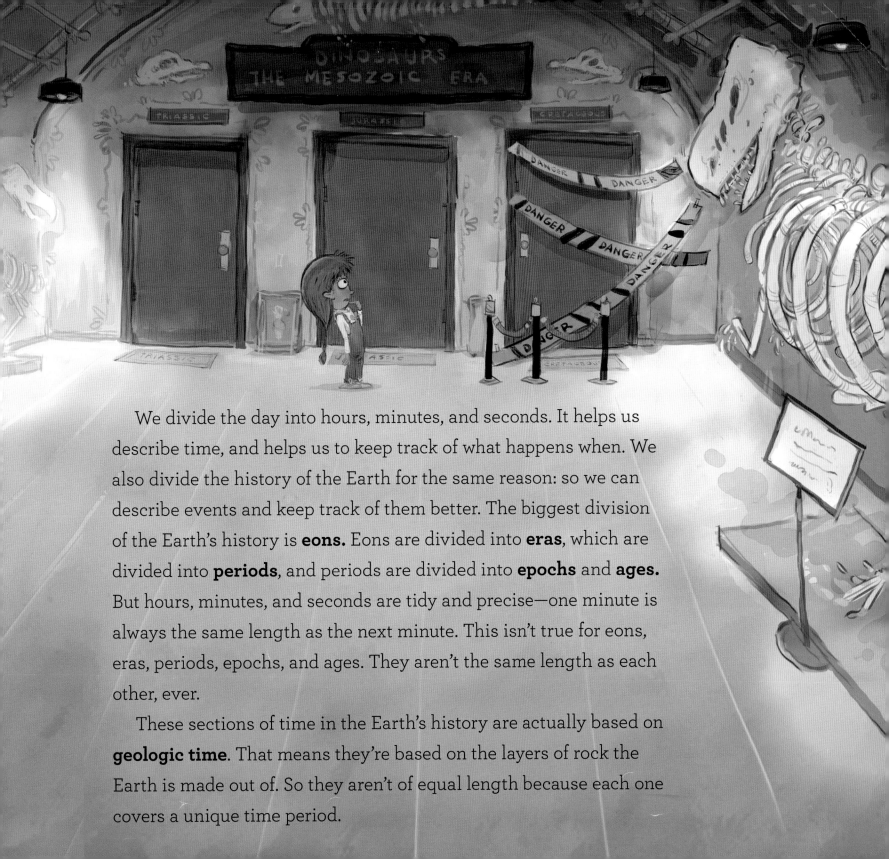

We divide the day into hours, minutes, and seconds. It helps us describe time, and helps us to keep track of what happens when. We also divide the history of the Earth for the same reason: so we can describe events and keep track of them better. The biggest division of the Earth's history is **eons.** Eons are divided into **eras**, which are divided into **periods**, and periods are divided into **epochs** and **ages.** But hours, minutes, and seconds are tidy and precise—one minute is always the same length as the next minute. This isn't true for eons, eras, periods, epochs, and ages. They aren't the same length as each other, ever.

These sections of time in the Earth's history are actually based on **geologic time**. That means they're based on the layers of rock the Earth is made out of. So they aren't of equal length because each one covers a unique time period.

Dinosaurs walked the Earth during the **Mesozoic** era. The Mesozoic era had three periods: the **Triassic**, the **Jurassic**, and the **Cretaceous**. Each of these periods was tens of millions of years long. Dinosaurs were around for over a hundred million years. Humans haven't even been around for half a million years!

The three geological time periods the dinosaurs lived in were not all the same. The planet was a very different place at the beginning of the Triassic from how it was at the end of the Cretaceous. And the dinosaurs who lived then were very different, too.

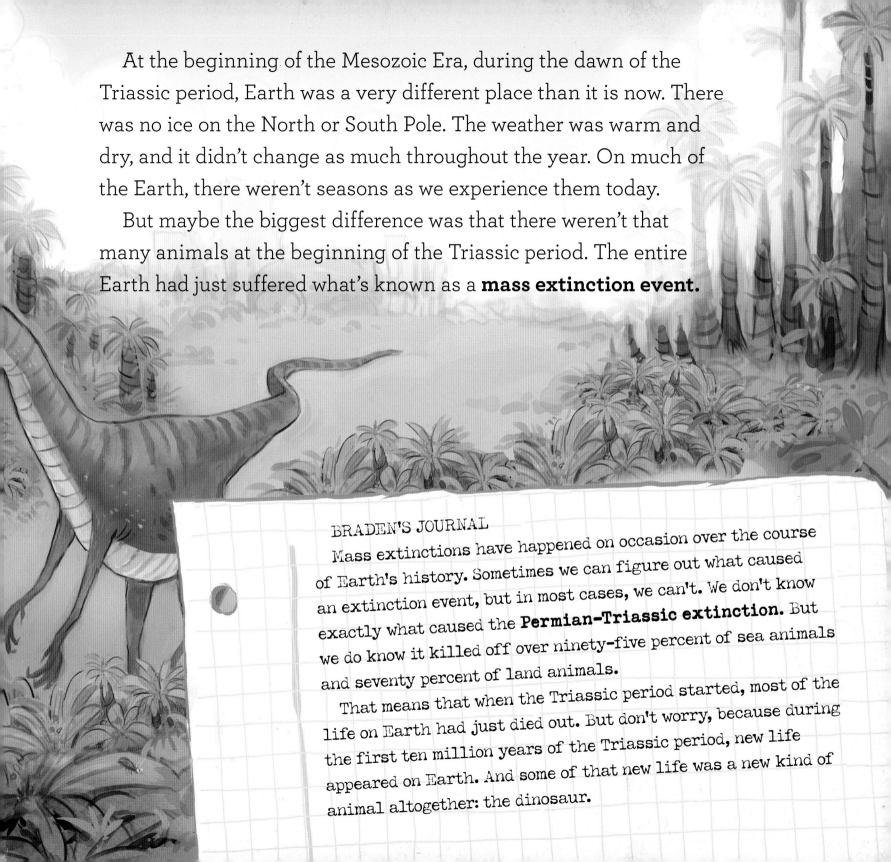

At the beginning of the Mesozoic Era, during the dawn of the Triassic period, Earth was a very different place than it is now. There was no ice on the North or South Pole. The weather was warm and dry, and it didn't change as much throughout the year. On much of the Earth, there weren't seasons as we experience them today.

But maybe the biggest difference was that there weren't that many animals at the beginning of the Triassic period. The entire Earth had just suffered what's known as a **mass extinction event.**

BRADEN'S JOURNAL

Mass extinctions have happened on occasion over the course of Earth's history. Sometimes we can figure out what caused an extinction event, but in most cases, we can't. We don't know exactly what caused the **Permian-Triassic extinction.** But we do know it killed off over ninety-five percent of sea animals and seventy percent of land animals.

That means that when the Triassic period started, most of the life on Earth had just died out. But don't worry, because during the first ten million years of the Triassic period, new life appeared on Earth. And some of that new life was a new kind of animal altogether: the dinosaur.

If you could see Earth from space during the Triassic period, you might not even recognize it! The familiar shapes of North and South America wouldn't have been there. Or Europe, or Africa, or Asia. During the Triassic, all the land on Earth was bunched up in one supercontinent called **Pangaea**, and there was only one giant ocean.

After spending a few minutes observing life in the Triassic period, the kids return to the Science Museum. It's time to jump forward almost *fifty million years* and see what things are like in the Jurassic period!

BRADEN'S JOURNAL
The Triassic period was over fifty million years long. And that was just the first period of dinosaur life on the planet! Compared to the dinosaurs, we're babies.

As the Jurassic period went on, the supercontinent Pangaea began to break up. Europe and Asia split apart from North America, and South America began to separate from Africa. Smaller sections of land were now surrounded by many oceans. The climate shifted: the Triassic had been hot and dry, but the Jurassic was hot and wet. Life flourished in the seas, and on land as well. Many new species of dinosaurs appeared . . . and many new species of other kinds of animals did, too.

BRADEN'S JOURNAL

The earliest birds appeared during the Jurassic period. This one, **archaeopteryx,** is thought by scientists to be one of the very first birds ever. You can recognize it as a bird even though modern birds look very different. That's what hundreds of millions of years of **evolution** will do!

By the way, birds weren't the only ones with feathers back then. Scientists now think lots of dinosaurs had them, too, even dinosaurs that didn't fly.

As the years passed and the Triassic period gave way to the Jurassic period, dinosaurs evolved from their early beginnings into the shapes we're more used to seeing. Many familiar dinosaurs walked the Earth during the Jurassic period. **Sauropods** like giant **brachiosaurus** and **diplodocus** ate lush vegetation that they reached with their long necks. **Predators** like **allosaurus** hunted and ate smaller dinosaurs.

During the Cretaceous period, the continents continued to drift apart. As they moved, the map of the world began to look more like how it looks now. The continents spread farther and farther apart, and Earth got colder and colder. The weather in the Cretaceous period was cold compared to the Jurassic and Triassic periods. Toward the end of the Cretaceous period, the continents finally began to settle into positions close to where they stand today.

The Cretaceous period was a golden age for dinosaurs—new types of dinosaurs appeared constantly. Their populations were dense, too. Many dinosaurs, such as iguanodons, traveled in giant herds.

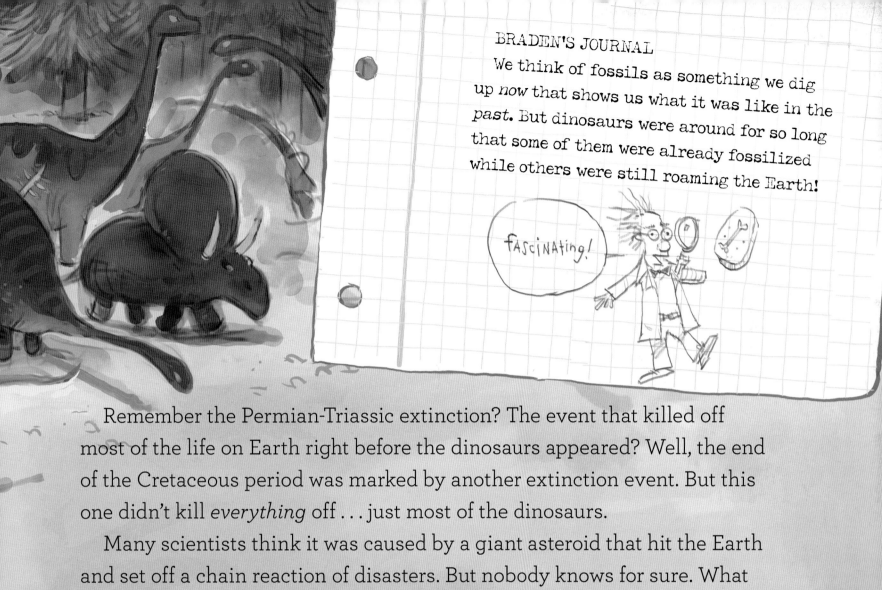

Remember the Permian-Triassic extinction? The event that killed off most of the life on Earth right before the dinosaurs appeared? Well, the end of the Cretaceous period was marked by another extinction event. But this one didn't kill *everything* off . . . just most of the dinosaurs.

Many scientists think it was caused by a giant asteroid that hit the Earth and set off a chain reaction of disasters. But nobody knows for sure. What we do know is that the only dinosaurs who survived the **Cretaceous-Tertiary extinction** were avian dinosaurs—the birdlike ones.

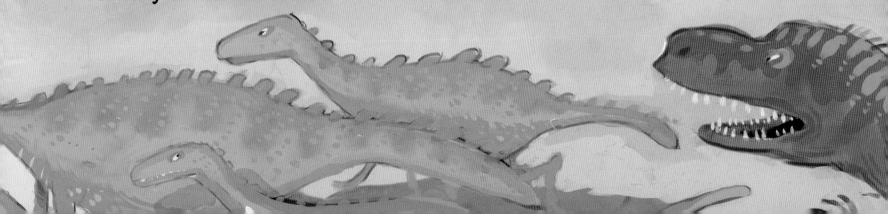

SATURDAY
9:59 A.M.

So, just as the clock ticked toward ten a.m., the investigators shooed Tiny back through the door to the Jurassic period.

Looking at dinosaur skeletons in a museum is very different from having living dinosaurs right in front of you to study. You don't know how big their muscles were or what color their skin was, or if they had feathers. Paleontologists only have skeletons to work from, so they have to make a lot of informed guesses. Examining bones is the closest a paleontologist will ever get to going back to the Triassic, Jurassic, or Cretaceous Periods. The investigators were very lucky today—they were more like **zoologists** than paleontologists, at least for a little while.

We'll never know for sure, but it's possible that Tiny—or one of his species—is in this very room, as a fossilized skeleton.

Compsognathus. Amazing!

Experiment: Create Your Own Archaeological Dig!

Important: Do this experiment with the help of an adult!

In this experiment, you get to dig up a fossil and experience the excitement of discovery that real-life archaeologists do as part of their jobs.

In this project, you will:

1. Make your own fossils.
2. Bury the fossils under layers of dirt and sand to create an "archaeological dig site."
3. Trade sites with your friends, dig up the fossils, and use careful observation to determine what the fossil is and where it came from!

The Experiment:

You will need:

Assistance

- an adult (important!)

Fossil dough

- 4 cups of flour
- 1 cup of salt
- 1.5 cups of water

Fossil Artifacts

- small dinosaur toys
- plant leaves
- shells from the beach
- leftover bones from cooking, such as chicken or fish bones

Archaeological dig site

- ample dry sand
- small amount of water
- baking pan or baking dish at least 2" deep

Digging tool suggestions

- scraping tools, such as a flat-head screwdriver or small trowel
- stiff-bristled brush
- old toothbrush
- toothpicks for details

Stage 1: Making the Fossils

1. Mix together the flour, salt, and water. Work the mix into dough.
2. Roll onto a cookie sheet with dough approximately ½" thick, or pat into flat circles also approximately ½" thick.
3. Make a fossil impression using your artifacts!
   a. With a dinosaur toy, try pushing it into the dough sideways. You could also use it to make footprints.
   b. With your hand, try making a W with your fingers to make a three-toed dinosaur foot impression.
   c. If using a leaf, see how well you can imprint its fine details into the dough. Get creative and add details.
4. Parental guidance necessary! Bake the fossils on a cookie sheet at 350 degrees F for one hour and remove.

If you are working in a pair or a group and plan to bury your fossils for friends to dig up, you may wish to keep your fossils a surprise!

Stage 2: Burying and Digging Up the Fossils

Now it's time to investigate!

1. Mix together the additional sand with a very small amount of water (approximately 10 parts sand, 1 part water).
2. Compress a layer of sand into your baking sheet.
3. Bury your fossils, using your hands to squish the sand down hard on top.
4. Trade "archaeological dig sites" with a friend and start excavating! Be sure to be very careful when digging in the sand. Just like real archaeologists, you don't want to damage the delicate fossils underneath! *Can you correctly identify the fossils you discover?*

Investigation and Discussion

As you begin to dig up the fossils, go slowly. How little do you have to uncover to be able identify what the fossil is? Archaeologists often have to piece together puzzles and mysteries without ever seeing a complete skeleton, plant, or marine fossil. What clues can you use as you dig to learn about the fossil without even seeing the whole thing?

If you made some impression fossils, how much of the detail transferred? Did the impression of your toy look just like the real thing, or was some of the detail lost? This happens in real life as well. Under the tremendous pressure and heat of being underground for millions of years, even strong bones don't always hold up perfectly. But still, fossils are amazing to look at. Next time you see one, imagine how much more detail and richness the original animal or plant had when it was alive!

Past and Future

Digging up and studying fossils isn't just fun, it's important. By carefully studying plant and animal fossils, along with the rocks that surround them, we can learn a lot about what the Earth was like long ago—and more important, what happened over time as things changed. What we learn from those investigations helps us understand the way the Earth is changing now, and what life might be like in the future!

—Nate

GLOSSARY

AGE
A unit of geologic time, loosely defined as millions of years.

ALLOSAURUS
A meat-eating dinosaur from the late Jurassic Period. It lived in North America, was about thirty feet long, and weighed about three thousand pounds.

ARCHAEOPTERYX
A birdlike, meat-eating dinosaur from the late Jurassic Period. It lived in Europe, was about twenty inches long, and weighed approximately two pounds.

BRACHIOSAURUS
A plant-eating dinosaur from the mid to late Jurassic Period. It lived in North America and Europe and was one of the largest dinosaurs ever discovered. It was eighty-two feet long and weighed approximately sixty-two tons.

CARNIVOROUS
Feeding on meat.

CRETACEOUS
A geologic period approximately 140 million to sixty-five million years ago.

CRETACEOUS-TERTIARY EXTINCTION
A global extinction event that occurred at the boundary of the Cretaceous Period and the Paleogene Period, responsible for eliminating approximately eighty percent of all species of animals, including nearly all dinosaurs.

DIPLODOCUS
A plant-eating dinosaur from the late Jurassic Period. It was about ninety feet long and weighed about 115 tons.

EON
A unit of geologic time, loosely defined as approximately a half billion years or more.

EPOCH
A unit of geologic time, loosely defined as tens of millions of years.

ERA
A unit of geologic time, loosely defined as several hundred million years.

EVOLUTION
A gradual change over many generations in the characteristics of a plant or animal species.

FOSSIL
Any trace of a living thing, such as a skeleton or footprint, from a past geologic age.

GEOLOGIC TIME
A relative way of dividing large periods of time. The largest unit of geologic time is a supereon. Supereons can be divided into eons, which can be divided into eras and then reduced down to periods, epochs, and ages.

JURASSIC
A geologic period approximately 190 to 140 million years ago.

MASS EXTINCTION EVENT
A quick, widespread decrease of the amount of life on Earth.

MESOZOIC
The period of time from 250 to sixty-five million years ago.

NON-AVIAN
Not related to birds.

PALEONTOLOGIST
A scientist who studies life forms existing in prehistoric times.

PALEONTOLOGY
The study of the geologic past, often through the study of fossils.

PANGAEA
A supercontinent that existed in the early Mesozoic era.

PERIOD
A unit of geologic time, loosely defined as between ten and one hundred million years.

PERMIAN-TRIASSIC EXTINCTION
A global extinction event that occurred during the latter part of the Permian Period, responsible for eliminating over ninety-five percent of marine and seventy percent of terrestrial species.

PREDATOR
Any animal that is carnivorous, or eats meat.

SAUROPOD
A type of dinosaur with a long neck, long tail, small head, and four thick legs, most notable for their enormous size.

TRIASSIC
A geologic period approximately 250 to 200 million years ago.

TYRANNOSAURUS REX
A meat-eating dinosaur from the Cretaceous period. It was forty feet long and weighed about ten tons.

ZOOLOGIST
A scientist who studies animals, both living and extinct.